Ab Sheets

These fifteen acti to the following stories of Ancient Rome:

<u>Cheating at the Games</u>
Milo and Marius are competing in the chariot race at the Spring games but someone is trying to fix the result.

<u>The Fish-Trap</u>
The Emperor has lost his ring and Flavia and her friend are accused of stealing it. They must find the real culprit before it is too late.

<u>The Tortoise and the Eagle</u>
The Roman army is attacking a British town when the standard-bearer is wounded and the army loses heart. Can Cato save the day?

These stories appear in
HISTORY QUICK READS: ANCIENT ROME by David Oakden
published by Anglia Young Books, ISBN 1-904936-11-3

There are five photocopiable sheets to accompany each story and they include a wide range of differentiated activities, from the very simple to the more complex, so that pupils can work at their own level. Many of the activities have a strong literacy element and the aim is to appeal to children of every ability, giving them a taste of the historical period and reinforcing and extending what they have learnt from reading the stories.

Name Date

Cheating at the Games

The Romans enjoyed sports and games. Use the words at the bottom of the page to complete these sentences.

1. Roman athletes threw the ________ and the ________.
2. Roman athletes would ______ and _________ in competitions.
3. Roman fighters would __________ to see who was the strongest.
4. Roman soldiers raced their ____________.
5. Roman people went to the ____________ to see the competitions.
6. Roman people liked to make _______ on the results of the races.

bets	**stadium**	**javelin**	**chariots**
discus	**run**	**wrestle**	**jump**

Name Date

Cheating at the Games

The most famous Roman stadium is the Colosseum in Rome. Use the Internet to find a picture of the building, and draw it here.

Name two things that happened in this stadium in Roman times:

____

____

Now think of something you have seen in a stadium, and write down what you saw. (**Clue: you might have seen it on television.**)

____

Name Date

Cheating at the Games

Label the soldier's uniform.

sandals	**sword**	**helmet**	**cloak**	**leg guards**
shoulder plates	**woollen tunic**	**body armour**		

Name Date

Cheating at the Games

These towns were important to the Romans:

- Colchester
- Exeter
- London
- York
- Worcester

Put the towns on this map of Great Britain and then use the Internet to find out what the towns were called in Roman times.

- Colchester was called ____________________
- Exeter was called ________________________
- London was called ________________________
- York was called __________________________
- Worcester was called ____________________

The letters HW are on the map. Find out what they mean.

____

Name Date

Now try this word search.

Cheating at the Games

w	s	j	s	t	a	d	i	u	m
d	r	e	a	t	a	d	b	w	l
e	i	e	s	v	a	s	e	o	e
s	d	s	s	t	e	b	t	o	a
t	i	j	c	t	e	l	l	d	v
l	e	f	c	u	l	r	i	e	e
h	o	r	s	e	s	i	c	n	s
s	o	l	d	i	e	r	n	e	e
t	r	i	b	u	n	e	a	g	m
c	h	a	r	i	o	t	o	y	e

Words to find:

bet, chariot, discus, horses, javelin, leaves, sesterce, soldier, stables, stadium, tribune, wooden, wrestling.

Name Date

The Fish-Trap

Flavia goes to help in the kitchen. Here are some of the jobs she might have to do.

- grind wheat to make flour
- make bread
- chop herbs and vegetables
- wash dishes
- preserve food

Choose one of these activities and write down how you think the job would be done in Roman times. Remember there were few metal objects in the kitchen and no modern machines. For some ideas, Google **Ancient Rome/Roman Food**.

___

___

___

How would you do the same job in your kitchen?

___

___

___

Name Date

The Fish-Trap

This shows Roman people enjoying a feast. Put yourself somewhere in this picture. You can be a servant or you can be someone eating the food.

In this picture of a feast I am

____.

Name Date

The Fish-Trap

In this story, Danta is the Emperor's cook. She makes three meals each day. To find out about Roman meals, go on to the Internet **(Ask.com/The Romans - Food)**.

Write down what you had for breakfast yesterday

____

Now write down what Danta might make for the first meal

____

Write down what you had in the middle of the day

____

Now write down what Danta might make for the second meal

____

Write down what you had for your evening meal

____

Now write down what Danta might make for the last meal

____

Name Date

The Fish-Trap

Romans liked to wear rings. Sometimes rich people wore a ring on each finger.

Either draw the snake-shaped ring mentioned in the story or search on the Internet for **Ancient Roman Finger Rings** and make a copy of a different ring.

Name Date

Now try this word search.

The Fish-Trap

f	k	n	s	g	s	t	w	e	s	d	p
r	m	i	n	o	e	l	l	i	e	l	o
e	d	i	t	k	l	b	a	d	n	n	c
e	r	i	c	c	a	d	d	v	e	e	k
d	f	u	n	t	h	a	i	t	e	e	e
o	b	l	e	i	p	e	t	e	g	s	t
m	c	g	o	e	n	o	n	a	r	m	p
l	e	o	k	w	r	g	i	c	a	o	r
v	c	a	o	i	e	r	n	o	t	n	i
s	n	l	l	k	r	r	n	m	t	e	s
s	e	r	v	a	n	t	s	b	l	y	o
r	o	o	m	c	o	u	c	h	e	s	n

Words to find:

bucket, comb, cook, couches, dining, flower, freedom, kitchen, marriage, meal, money, padded, pocket, prison, rattle, ring, room, rotten, servants, slaves, snake, soldier, vegetable, wine.

Name Date

The Tortoise and the Eagle

Using the words below, finish these sentences about the catapult.

The catapult was a large ____ ____________.

The soldiers ______________ it to the walls of a __________.

The soldiers put ____________ and burning ___________ into the catapult.

The rocks broke the _______________.

The arrows set ________ to ____________ doors and windows.

When the soldiers used the _____________ towns usually _________________.

wooden	**rocks**
walls	**arrows**
catapult	**war**
town	**machine**
fire	**surrendered**
dragged	

Name Date

The Tortoise and the Eagle

Roman Roads

The Romans built many roads in Britain. They made them straight so that soldiers could walk easily from place to place. Look at this diagram.

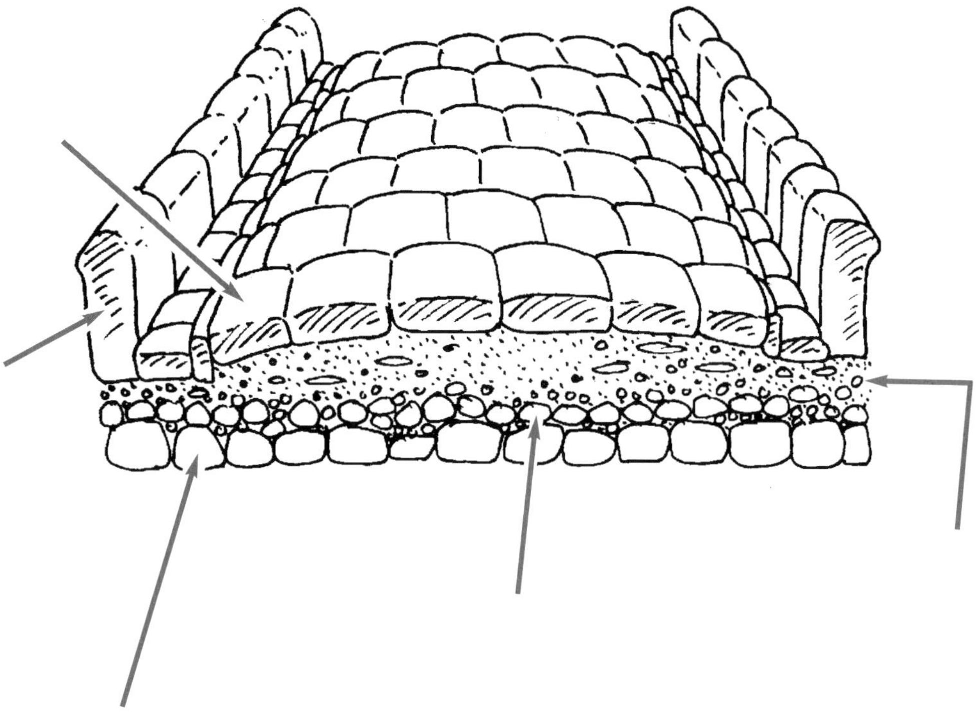

Now write these sentences next to the right arrows

Cement mixed with broken tiles

A layer of big stones at the bottom

Broken stones and pebbles

Kerb stones to drain away the water

Paving stones for a flat surface

Name Date

The Tortoise and the Eagle

This is the way Roman people counted. Our numbers are underneath the Roman numbers.

I	II	III	IV	V	VI	VII	VIII	IX	X
1	2	3	4	5	6	7	8	9	10
XI	XX	XXX	XL	L	LX	LXX	LXXX	XC	C
11	20	30	40	50	60	70	80	90	100

Now complete this 100 square using Roman numbers.

I									X
XI									XX
									L
	LII								
									C

Now try to write your age in Roman numbers ________

Name Date

The Tortoise and the Eagle

The Tortoise

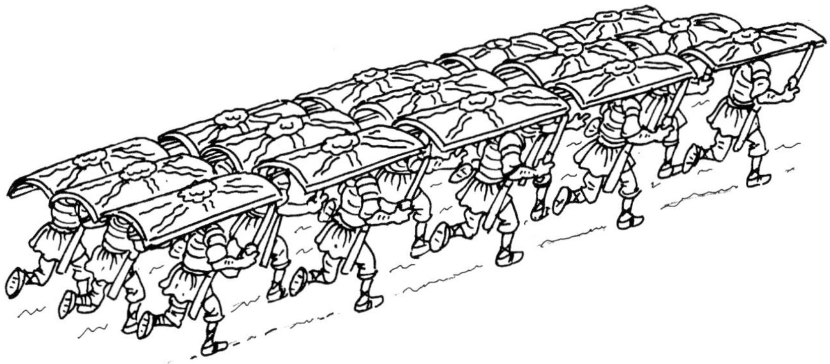

This is a picture of the 'tortoise' in the story. Imagine you are a soldier and think of 3 rules that you must obey to make certain that the 'tortoise' works.

1. ______________________________

2. ______________________________

3. ______________________________

Cato helps the soldiers by picking up the standard. Draw your own standard here.

Name Date

Now try this word search.

The Tortoise and the Eagle

c	s	b	a	t	t	l	e	l
t	a	t	c	a	m	p	a	e
o	e	t	a	b	e	e	r	g
r	p	a	a	n	d	l	m	i
t	o	m	g	p	d	l	o	o
o	e	t	a	l	u	a	u	n
i	l	a	u	r	e	l	r	i
s	b	e	a	r	e	r	t	d
e	m	p	i	r	e	l	e	e

Words to find:

armour, battle, bearer, beer, camp, catapult, eagle, empire, laurel, legion, standard, tortoise.